The One and Only

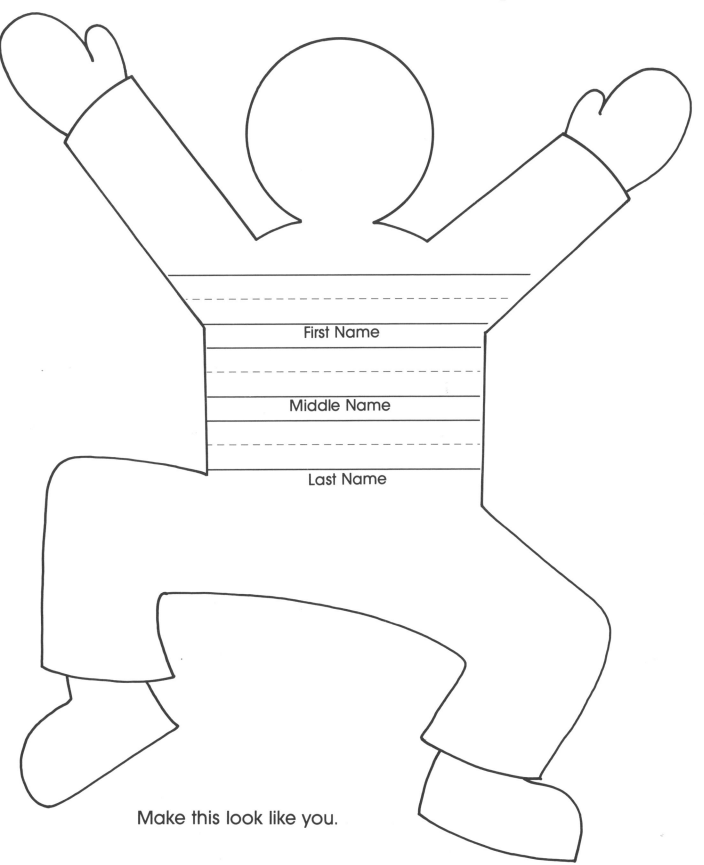

First Name

Middle Name

Last Name

Make this look like you.

My Description

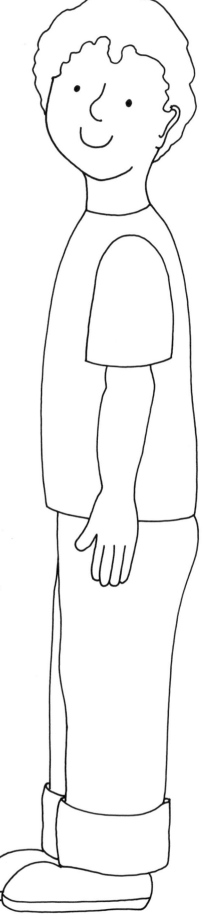

I have _____ hair.
color

My eyes are _____.
color

My skin is _____.
color

I am _____ inches tall.
number

I weigh _____ pounds.
number

I am a _____.
girl or boy

I am _____ handed.
right or left

I have lost _____ baby teeth.

I have dimples.   yes   no

More facts about _____

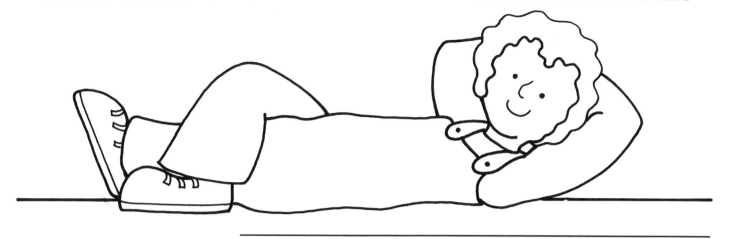

1. My full name is: _____

2. My age is _____

3. My birthdate is _____

4. My house number is _____

   on _____

   in the city of _____

   in the state of _____

   in the country _____

5. My phone number is _____

     Discoveries About Me

Design a T-shirt just for you.

1. Add your initials or nickname.
2. Draw a picture that shows what you like to do.
   Use your favorite colors.

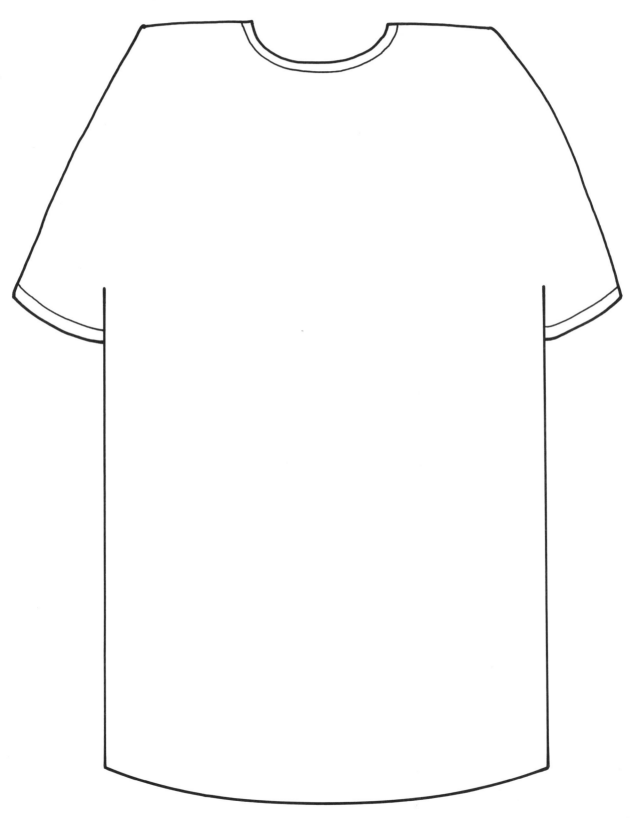

 Discoveries About Me

My Footprints on _____
date

1. Take off your shoes and socks.
2. Trace each foot carefully in the correct box.

Left foot   **Right foot**

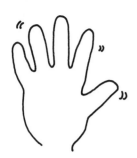

My fingerprints are *unique!

*one of a kind

1. Trace your hands.
2. Place your fingerprints at the end of each finger. (Use a stamp pad.)

Left hand

Right hand

Discoveries About Me

My Talents and Dreams

I am already good at . . .

1. _____

2. _____

3. _____

I'm learning how to . . .

1. _____

2. _____

3. _____

Someday I hope to be able to . . .

1. _____

2. _____

3. _____

                   Discoveries About Me

My family name is _____

My family likes to do many things together. Here are some things we do.

1. _____

2. _____

3. _____

See the _____ family work together.

See the _____ family play together.

Name _____

Birthday Bear

Light up Bear's birthday cake. Cut and paste flames above the rhyming candles.

star

frog

shell

bee

fish

top

hat

box

HAPPY BIRTHDAY, BEAR!

sea

mop

dog

cat

fox

car

dish

bell

Background for the Teacher:

Cute, loveable, huggable Teddy Bears in many varieties and sizes are irresistible to young and old alike. Teddy Bears are enjoying a new wave of popularity. People collect old teddy bears, buy new ones, dig out their old, treasured bear friends and remember the warmth and security of childhood.

Teddy Bears have been a part of childhood since the early 1900's. When President Theodore Roosevelt refused to shoot a helpless bear on a 1902 hunting expedition, the Teddy Bear was born. Roosevelt's deed was immortalized by a political cartoon in The Washington Post. The cartoon pictured an appealing bear cub. A New York shopkeeper began making toy stuffed bears and asked permission to call them Teddy's Bears. The bears were an instant success and led to the creation of the Ideal Novelty and Toy Company.

The Teddy Bear boom spread to Germany where the Steiff Company became famous for producing thousands of plush brown bears.

Since then, Teddy Bears have been a favorite toy with millions sold each year.

Extension Activities:

● Make a Teddy Bear display with examples of bears on stickers, gift wrap, books, food, toys and other items.
● Have a Teddy Bear Day when students can bring in their favorite bears or other stuffed animals. Serve Jelly Bears or cut-out bear cookies.
● Read books about Teddy Bears or other loveable storybook bears such as:
Winnie the Pooh
The Berenstain Bears
A Pocket for Corduroy

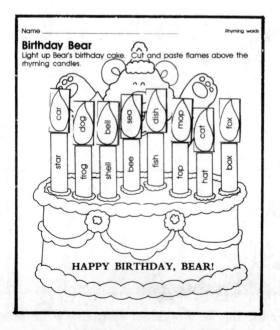

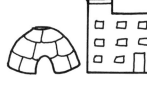 # Where I live

This is the house where the _____
family lives.

Draw your house.
Make a window for each person in your family.
Draw each person in a different window.
Don't forget yourself.

_____ 's Family Tree

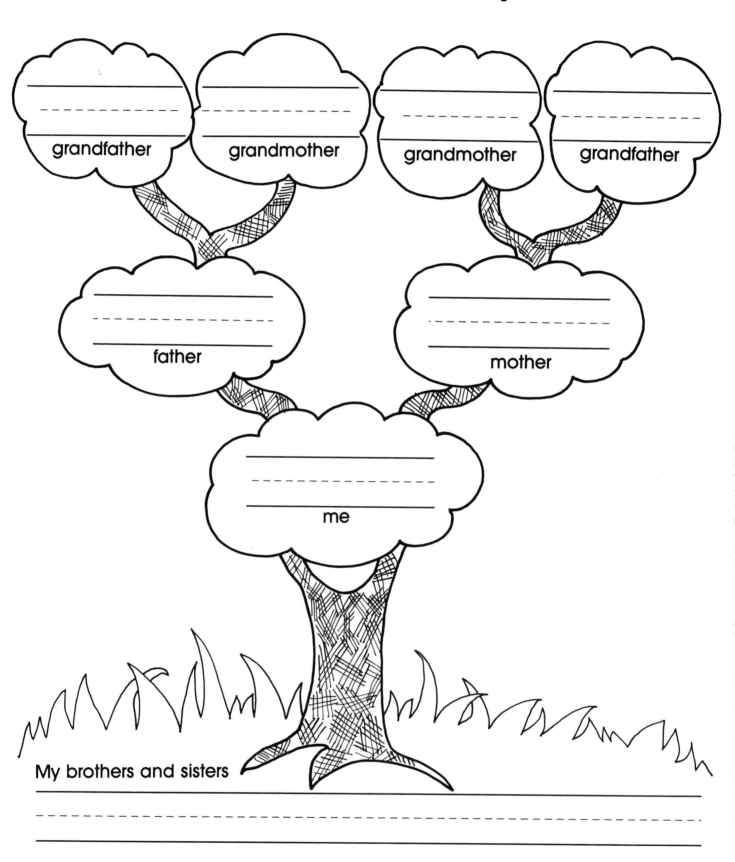

grandfather   grandmother   grandmother   grandfather

father   mother

me

My brothers and sisters

Find the Family

```
s o n a g f p e d s y i d
b t s g r c o u s i n j a
u p z f a i z e y s f m u
c a q u n c l e j t k k g
g r a n d m o t h e r x h
d e r t f o n h h r l q t
v n d o a t e m r w g n e
e t q u t h a n h i g w r
y s m l h e u e n k l k c
f a t h e r n p d f h v b
b v g b r o t h e r c c x
p w a j t s a e s p m b u
n i e c e o n w z r o l a
```

father   cousin   grandmother
mother   nephew   grandfather
sister   niece   aunt
brother   daughter   uncle
parents   son

My Friends

I like many people. Some people are special to me. I call those people my friends.

Here are the names of some of my friends.

1. _____

2. _____

3. _____

4. _____

5. _____

6. _____

Discoveries About Me

Draw you and your friends.

My friends and I like to

_____

- -

_____

- -

_____

- -

We don't like to

_____

- -

_____

- -

_____

- -

Sometimes I do things because my friends do them, but most of the time I make my own choices.

_____

- 's Pets

_____

The pets I already have are:

_____   _____   _____

- - - - - - - - - - -   - - - - - - - - - - -   - - - - - - - - - - -

_____   _____   _____

My pets look like this:

I feed my pets _____.

My pets sleep in a _____.

My pets can do tricks.   yes   no

If I could have a new pet, I would get a _____.

It would look like this:

I would name it _____.

Toys

Now I like to play with

_____

- -

_____.

I have many toys.
My favorite toy when I was small was

_____

- -

_____.

If I could have a new toy, I would get

_____

- -

_____.

You can find toys in funny places.

I found _____ in the kitchen.

I use it to _____.

I found _____ in the garage.

I turned it into a _____.

I found _____ in the yard.

It became _____.

My Most Favorite Things

1. My favorite color is _____.

2. The T.V. show I like most is _____.

3. The best tasting foods are _____, _____ _____ _____, _____ and _____.

4. I like to read books about _____, _____ _____ and _____.

5. My favorite song is _____.

6. The sport I like best is _____.

7. I like to go to _____ on my vacation, so that I can _____.

 Discoveries About Me

My Least Favorite Things

1. I don't like the color _____.

   It makes me think of _____.

2. The food I really hate is _____

   because _____.

3. The worst show on T.V. is _____.

4. I really don't like books about _____.

5. The song that drives me crazy is _____.

6. The game I hate to play is _____.

7. I would never go to _____

on my vacation.

 Discoveries About Me

When _____ Was Small

When I was only one year old . . .

I couldn't

1. --

2. --

3. --

I was able to

1. --

2. --

3. --

I looked like this.

When _____ Grows Up

When I am grown . . .

I will be able to

1. _____

2. _____

3. _____

I won't be able to

1. _____

2. _____

3. _____

I think I will look like this.

I Remember

The **best** thing that has happened to me so far . . .

_____

- -

_____

- -

_____

- -

_____

- -

_____

- -

_____

The **worst** thing that ever happened to me . . .

_____

- -

_____

- -

_____

- -

_____

- -

_____

My Measurements

Use a tape measure and a friend
to find these measurements.

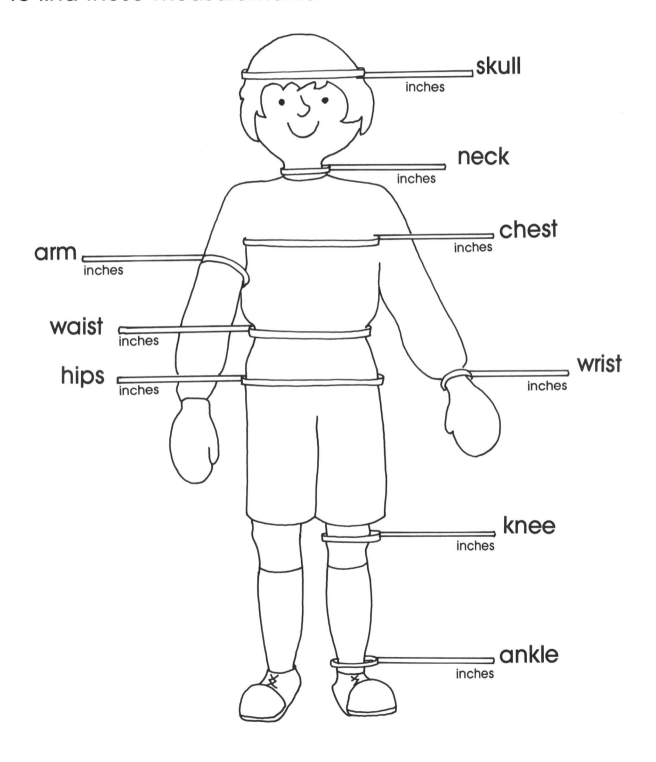

skull ____ inches

neck ____ inches

chest ____ inches

arm ____ inches

waist ____ inches

hips ____ inches

wrist ____ inches

knee ____ inches

ankle ____ inches

Discoveries About Me

My Growth Diary

Save this paper.
Use a tape measure to see how tall you have grown.
Write the inches in the box.
Write the date, too.

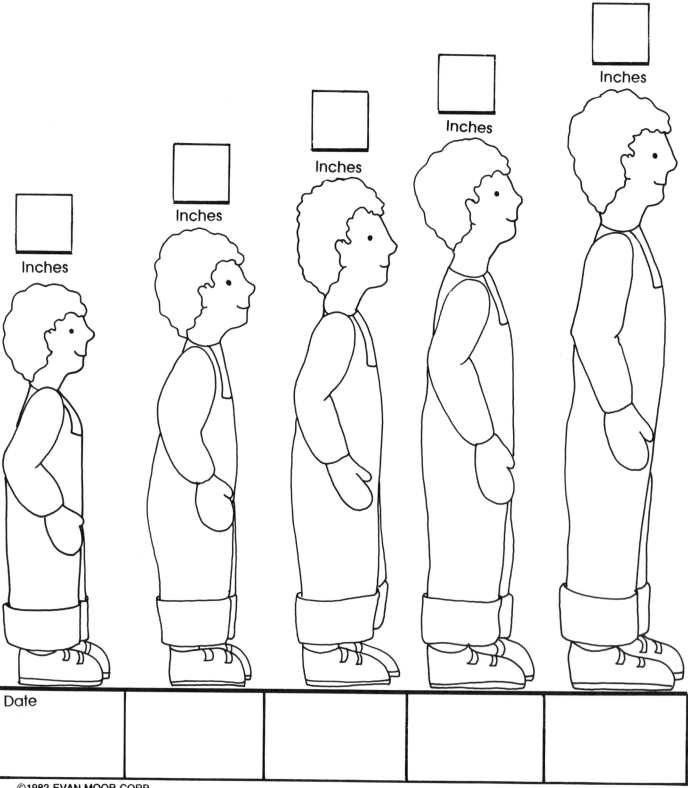

Inches

Inches

Inches

Inches

Inches

Date

Discoveries About Me

It's wonderful to be
The one and only **ME!**

There is no one else in the whole world exactly like me. I am unique. That means I'm one of a kind. I like myself for many reasons. Some of the reasons are

Discoveries About Me

From my nose to my toes
From my chin to my shin
There is no one exactly like Me
From here at my waist
To my "sit-upon" place
There is no one exactly like Me
Tho' you search far and near
I know you will find
There is no one like Me
I'm one of a kind.

J. E. Moore